Poodles Don't Do Dishes

By **Tilly Hutton**

Illustrations By **Mark Grundig**

Hutton Electronic Publishing   Westport

Poodles Don't Do Dishes

Copyright 2007 by

Caroline DuBois Hutton

ISBN # 0-9785171-5-6

Published by
Huttonelectronicpublishing.com
160 Compo Road N., Westport, CT 06880-2102
Manufactured in the United States of America

*A portion of the proceeds of this book
will go to further the work of
Best Friends Animal Sanctuary
in Kanab, Utah.*

Poodles don't do dishes.

...Or take out the garbage.

Poodles don't vacuum

Or dust

Or do windows.

Poodles don't make beds for other people...

Though they do make their own beds.

Poodles don't cook.

Though they love to eat. Some of their favorite dishes are

Filet Mignon

And lobster

And those little black eggs that are so salty.

Poodles don't bathe themselves...though they spend a lot of time at the beauty parlor.

It has been said that other dogs, seeing the fantastic haircuts poodles sport, think they are a weird, religious sect.

They don't do their own nails;
  They have them done professionally.

(They have a manicurist for their front paws
  and a pedicurist for their back ones.)

Here are some things poodles Do do (yes, that too):

They go poodling...

To Chanel

And Bergdorf

And Tiffany.

Poodles preen.

They have wardrobes for all occasions, and they love to dress up and go to parties where they drink cosmopolitans and are very amusing.

They have good hair days...

and bad hair days.

Poodles like to nudge their toys with their pointy noses;

ditto, humans, for a pat or a stomach scratch.

Poodles love holidays...

Thanksgiving

Christmas

Easter

25

Poodles don't chase cars

*But they love to ride in them,
especially when they are going to the beach for the day.*

Poodles love sports events and are natural athletes.

Poodles are good at Yoga

Especially the 'downward dog' position.

Poodles are good at lying in laps.

And on peoples' beds (ahem, their beds)

Poodles bounce

And jounce

And snort

And cavort.

Poodles are good at barking,

Especially at the mailman.

Poodles are the clowns of the dog world.

Poodles love to garden

When the spirit moves them.

In the hierarchy of a household,

Poodles are always at the top
(though in your household, of course, your pooch is top dog).

Poodles hearts are large, belying their size,

And they will love and adore only you...

Forever.

LaVergne, TN USA
17 January 2010
170305LV00005B